EASY AVOCADO COOKBOOK

50 DELICIOUS AVOCADO RECIPES

By
Chef Maggie Chow
Copyright © 2015 by Saxonberg Associates

Published by
BookSumo, a division of Saxonberg Associates
http://www.booksumo.com/

1

STAY TO THE END OF THE COOKBOOK AND RECEIVE....

I really appreciate when people, take the time to read all of my recipes.

So, as a gift for reading this entire cookbook you will receive a **massive collection of special recipes.**

Read to the end of and get my *Easy Specialty Cookbook Box Set for FREE*!

This box set includes the following:

1. *Easy Sushi Cookbook*
2. *Easy Dump Dinner Cookbook*
3. *Easy Beans Cookbook*

Remember this box set is about **EASY** cooking.

In the *Easy Sushi Cookbook* you will learn the easiest methods to prepare almost every type of Japanese Sushi i.e. *California Rolls, the Perfect Sushi Rice, Crab Rolls, Osaka Style Sushi*, and so many others.

Then we go on to *Dump Dinners.* Nothing can be easier than a Dump Dinner. In the *Easy Dump Dinner Cookbook* we will learn how to master our slow cookers and make some amazingly unique dinners that will take almost *no effort*.

Finally in the *Easy Beans Cookbook* we tackle one of my favorite side dishes: Beans. There are so many delicious ways to make Baked Beans and Bean Salads that I had to share them.

So stay till the end and then keep on cooking with my *Easy Specialty Cookbook Box Set*!

About the Author.

Maggie Chow is the author and creator of your favorite *Easy Cookbooks* and *The Effortless Chef Series*. Maggie is a lover of all things related to food. Maggie loves nothing more than finding new recipes, trying them out, and then making them her own, by adding or removing ingredients, tweaking cooking times, and anything to make the recipe not only taste better, but be easier to cook!

For a complete listing of all my books please see my author page.

INTRODUCTION

Welcome to *The Effortless Chef Series*! Thank you for taking the time to download the *Easy Avocado Cookbook*. Come take a journey with me into the delights of easy cooking. The point of this cookbook and all my cookbooks is to exemplify the effortless nature of cooking simply.

In this book we focus on Avocados. You will find that even though the recipes are simple, the taste of the dishes is quite amazing.

So will you join me in an adventure of simple cooking? If the answer is yes (and I hope it is) please consult the table of contents to find the dishes you are most interested in. Once you are ready jump right in and start cooking.

— Chef Maggie Chow

TABLE OF CONTENTS

ANY ISSUES? CONTACT ME

If you find that something important to you is missing from this book please contact me at maggie@booksumo.com.

I will try my best to re-publish a revised copy taking your feedback into consideration and let you know when the book has been revised with you in mind.

:)

— Chef Maggie Chow

LEGAL NOTES

Common Abbreviations

cup(s)	C.
tablespoon	tbsp
teaspoon	tsp
ounce	oz.
pound	lb

*All units used are standard American measurements

CHAPTER 1: EASY AVOCADO RECIPES

AVOCADO SALSA

Ingredients

- 1 mango, peeled, seeded and diced
- 1 avocado, peeled, pitted, and diced
- 4 medium tomatoes, diced
- 1 jalapeno pepper, seeded and diced
- 1/2 C. chopped fresh cilantro
- 3 cloves garlic, diced
- 1 tsp salt
- 2 tbsps fresh lime juice
- 1/4 C. chopped red onion

- 3 tbsps olive oil

Directions

- Get a bowl, mix: garlic, mango, cilantro, avocado, and tomatoes.
- Stir the mix then add in your olive oil, salt, red onions, and lime juice.
- Stir your salsa to evenly distribute the liquids. Then place a covering of plastic on the bowl and put everything in the fridge for 40 mins.
- Enjoy.

Amount per serving (6 total)

Timing Information:

Preparation	
Cooking	15 m
Total Time	45 m

Nutritional Information:

Calories	158 kcal
Fat	12 g
Carbohydrates	13.8g
Protein	1.9 g
Cholesterol	0 mg
Sodium	397 mg

* Percent Daily Values are based on a 2,000 calorie diet.

Sweet Avocado Snack

Ingredients

- 1 avocado, peeled and pitted
- 1/2 C. milk
- 1/4 C. white sugar
- 1/2 tsp vanilla extract

Directions

- Puree your avocados with a food processor until everything is smooth then combine in: the vanilla, sugar, and milk.
- Continue processing everything until it is all smooth again then place the mix in a bowl and place a covering of plastic on the bowl.
- Put everything in the fridge for 30 mins.
- Enjoy.

Amount per serving (4 total)

Timing Information:

Preparation	20 m
Cooking	20 m
Total Time	40 m

Nutritional Information:

Calories	146 kcal
Fat	8 g
Carbohydrates	18.3g
Protein	2 g
Cholesterol	2 mg
Sodium	16 mg

* Percent Daily Values are based on a 2,000 calorie diet.

Estillo Sarita

(Avocado Ceviche)

Ingredients

- 2 lbs large shrimp, peeled, deveined and chopped
- 3/4 C. fresh lime juice
- 5 roma (plum) tomatoes, diced
- 1 white onion, chopped
- 1/2 C. chopped fresh cilantro
- 1 tbsp Worcestershire sauce
- 1 tbsp ketchup
- 1 tsp hot pepper sauce
- salt and pepper to taste
- 1 avocado, peeled, pitted and diced
- 16 saltine crackers

Directions

- Get a bowl for your lime juice. Then add in the shrimp and stir everything. Leave the mix to sit for 10 mins.
- Now at this point the shrimp should be cooked.
- Add in: cilantro, tomatoes, and onions.
- Place a covering of plastic on the bowl and put everything in the fridge for 60 mins.
- Now add in: the pepper, Worcestershire, salt, hot sauce, and ketchup. Stir the ingredients into the sarita.
- When serving the dish place some shrimp on small platters.
- Enjoy.

Amount per serving (4 total)

Timing Information:

Preparation	
Cooking	1 h 30 m
Total Time	1 h 30 m

Nutritional Information:

Calories	352 kcal
Fat	10.9 g
Carbohydrates	24.3g
Protein	40.5 g
Cholesterol	346 mg
Sodium	1652 mg

* Percent Daily Values are based on a 2,000 calorie diet.

CLASSICAL HOMEMADE GUACAMOLE

Ingredients

- 3 avocados, peeled, pitted, and mashed
- 1 lime, juiced
- 1 tsp salt
- 1/2 C. diced onion
- 3 tbsps chopped fresh cilantro
- 2 roma (plum) tomatoes, diced
- 1 tsp diced garlic
- 1 pinch ground cayenne pepper

Directions

- Get a bowl, combine: salt, lime juice, and avocados.
- Stir the mix to evenly coat the avocadoes then combine in: the cayenne, onion, garlic, cilantro, and tomatoes.

- Place a covering of plastic on the bowl and put everything in the fridge for 60 mins.
- Enjoy.

Amount per serving (4 total)

Timing Information:

Preparation	
Cooking	10 m
Total Time	10 m

Nutritional Information:

Calories	262 kcal
Fat	22.2 g
Carbohydrates	18g
Protein	3.7 g
Cholesterol	0 mg
Sodium	596 mg

* Percent Daily Values are based on a 2,000 calorie diet.

Tomato and Avocado Soup

Ingredients

- 2 tbsps vegetable oil
- 1 (1 lb) package frozen pepper and onion veggie mix
- 2 cloves garlic, diced
- 3 tbsps ground cumin
- 1 (28 oz.) can crushed tomatoes
- 3 (4 oz.) cans chopped green chili peppers, drained
- 4 (14 oz.) cans vegetable broth
- salt and pepper to taste
- 1 (11 oz.) can whole kernel corn
- 12 oz. tortilla chips
- 1 C. shredded Cheddar cheese
- 1 avocado, peeled, pitted and diced

Directions

- Stir fry your onions and peppers for 2 mins in hot oil then add in the cumin and garlic. Continue frying the mix for 4 more mins until the veggies are soft.
- Now combine in the chili peppers and tomatoes.
- Stir the mix again and let the pepper cook for 30 secs before adding in some pepper, salt, and the broth.
- Now get everything boiling, set the heat to low, and let the mix gently simmer for 35 mins.
- Add in the corn to the mix and let the veggies cook for 7 mins.
- When serving the soup top each individual serving with some tortilla chips, avocado, and cheese.
- Enjoy.

Amount per serving (12 total)

Timing Information:

Preparation	15 m
Cooking	40 m
Total Time	55 m

Nutritional Information:

Calories	315 kcal
Fat	16.2 g
Carbohydrates	37.2g
Protein	8.7 g
Cholesterol	12 mg
Sodium	1152 mg

* Percent Daily Values are based on a 2,000 calorie diet.

MAGGIE'S EASY AVOCADO HONEY SALAD

Ingredients

- 2 tbsps white sugar
- 2 tbsps olive oil
- 4 tsps honey
- 1 tbsp cider vinegar
- 1 tsp lemon juice
- 2 C. torn salad greens
- 1 avocado, peeled, pitted and sliced
- 10 strawberries, sliced
- 1/2 C. chopped pecans

Directions

- Get a bowl, combine: lemon juice, sugar, vinegar, honey, and olive oil. Stir the mix until the sugar dissolves then place everything to the side.

- Get a 2nd decorative bowl and add in your greens.
- Add in your honey mix over the leaves and toss the salad to evenly coat the leaves with the dressing.
- Lay your strawberries and avocado pieces on top of the greens and coat everything with the pecans.
- Enjoy.

Amount per serving (2 total)

Timing Information:

Preparation	
Cooking	15 m
Total Time	15 m

Nutritional Information:

Calories	610 kcal
Fat	50 g
Carbohydrates	44g
Protein	6.1 g
Cholesterol	0 mg
Sodium	23 mg

* Percent Daily Values are based on a 2,000 calorie diet.

GINGER SOY SAUCE AVOCADO

Ingredients

- 1 avocado
- 1/2 tsp diced garlic
- 1/2 tsp diced fresh ginger root
- 1 tsp soy sauce

Directions

- Get a bowl, combine: soy sauce, ginger, and garlic.
- Let this mix sit for 10 mins then slice your avocado into two pieces.
- Remove the pit then top each of avocado with the sauce.
- Serve the avocado with a fork fresh.
- Enjoy.

Amount per serving (2 total)

Timing Information:

Preparation	
Cooking	10 m
Total Time	15 m

Nutritional Information:

Calories	14.7 g
Fat	9.1g
Carbohydrates	2.2 g
Protein	0 mg
Cholesterol	157 mg
Sodium	14.7 g

* Percent Daily Values are based on a 2,000 calorie diet.

164 kcal

Avocado Chiller

Ingredients

- 3 C. milk
- 1 avocado, peeled and pitted
- 4 tbsps white sugar

Directions

- Add the following to your blender and pulse the mix until it is smooth and resembles a thick milkshake: sugar, avocado and milk.
- Enjoy.

Amount per serving (3 total)

Timing Information:

Preparation	
Cooking	5 m
Total Time	5 m

Nutritional Information:

Calories	278 kcal
Fat	14.6 g
Carbohydrates	29.6g
Protein	9.4 g
Cholesterol	20 mg
Sodium	105 mg

* Percent Daily Values are based on a 2,000 calorie diet.

Avocado Appetizers

Ingredients

- 1 ripe avocado, peeled and pitted
- 1/2 C. fresh basil leaves
- 1 tbsp lime juice
- 1 clove garlic
- 1/4 tsp salt
- 1/4 tsp ground black pepper
- 1 cucumber, cut into 1/4-inch slices
- 1 plum tomato, cut into 1/4-inch slices
- 1 tbsp plain yogurt, or to taste

Directions

- Add the following to the bowl of a food processor: pepper, avocado, salt, basil, garlic, and lime juice.

- Pulse the mix until it is smooth then coat your pieces of cucumber with the avocado mix.
- Lay a piece of tomato over each one. Then top everything with your yogurt.
- Enjoy.

Amount per serving (4 total)

Timing Information:

Preparation	
Cooking	10 m
Total Time	10 m

Nutritional Information:

Calories	97 kcal
Fat	7.6 g
Carbohydrates	7.8g
Protein	1.9 g
Cholesterol	1 mg
Sodium	154 mg

* Percent Daily Values are based on a 2,000 calorie diet.

Avocado in the Morning

Ingredients

- 1/2 C. water
- 1/4 C. red quinoa
- 1 1/2 tsps olive oil
- 2 eggs
- 1 pinch salt and ground black pepper to taste
- 1/4 tsp seasoned salt
- 1/4 tsp ground black pepper
- 1 avocado, diced
- 2 tbsps crumbled feta cheese

Directions

- Get your quinoa boiling in water.
- Let the quinoa cook for 20 mins until it is fully done then drain any resulting liquids, if any exist.

- Now scramble your eggs in hot olive oil then top the eggs with some pepper and salt.
- Get a bowl, mix: feta, quinoa, and eggs.
- Stir the mix so that the eggs and cheese are evenly distributed throughout the quinoa then layer the mix with the avocado.
- Enjoy.

Amount per serving (2 total)

Timing Information:

Preparation	5 m
Cooking	20 m
Total Time	25 m

Nutritional Information:

Calories	372 kcal
Fat	26.8 g
Carbohydrates	24.1g
Protein	12.7 g
Cholesterol	194 mg
Sodium	379 mg

* Percent Daily Values are based on a 2,000 calorie diet.

Avocado Chiller II

Ingredients

- 1 avocado, peeled and pitted
- 1 C. orange juice
- 1/2 C. vanilla yogurt
- 5 ice cubes
- 4 frozen whole strawberries
- 1 tsp honey
- 1 tsp brown sugar
- 1 tsp flax seed meal

Directions

- Add the following to the bowl of a food processor: flax seed meal, avocado, honey, orange juice, strawberries, sugar, ice cubes, and vanilla yogurt.
- Pulse the mix for 2 mins.

- Enjoy.

Amount per serving (2 total)

Timing Information:

Preparation	
Cooking	10 m
Total Time	10 m

Nutritional Information:

Calories	298 kcal
Fat	16.4 g
Carbohydrates	36.1g
Protein	6.4 g
Cholesterol	3 mg
Sodium	51 mg

* Percent Daily Values are based on a 2,000 calorie diet.

Avocado Salad Dressing

Ingredients

- 1/2 C. avocado oil
- 1/4 C. olive oil
- 1/4 C. white vinegar
- 1 tsp lemon juice, or more to taste
- 1 tsp sesame oil, or more to taste
- 1 avocado, peeled, pitted, and coarsely chopped
- 4 cloves garlic, diced
- 1 tsp ground cumin
- salt and ground black pepper to taste

Directions

- Add the following to the bowl of a food processor: sesame oil, avocado oil, lemon juice, olive oil, and vinegar.

- Pulse the mix for 3 mins then combine in the avocado and continue pulsing everything for 3 more mins before adding in the cumin and garlic.
- Run the blender for about 2 more mins until you find the mix resembles a dressing.
- Now add in some pepper and salt.
- Place the dressing in a mason jar and place the lid on tightly.
- Put the dressing in the fridge until it is cold then shake everything before serving over a salad.
- Enjoy

Amount per serving (12 total)

Timing Information:

Preparation	
Cooking	10 m
Total Time	1 h 10 m

Nutritional Information:

Calories	153 kcal
Fat	16.5 g
Carbohydrates	1.9g
Protein	0.4 g
Cholesterol	0 mg
Sodium	15 mg

* Percent Daily Values are based on a 2,000 calorie diet.

THE BEST AVOCADO GAZPACHO

Ingredients

- 2 C. shredded zucchini
- 1 onion, coarsely chopped
- 1 avocado, peeled, pitted, and coarsely chopped
- 1/2 C. canned garbanzo beans, drained
- 1/4 C. apple cider vinegar
- 1 jalapeno pepper, seeded and diced
- 2 tsps lemon juice
- 1 clove garlic, smashed
- 1/4 tsp salt, or more to taste
- 1/4 tsp ground black pepper, or more to taste

Directions

- Get a bowl, mix: pepper, zucchini, salt, onions, garlic, avocado, lemon juice, garbanzo beans, jalapenos, and cider vinegar.
- Stir the mix to evenly distribute the ingredients. Then place a covering of plastic on the bowl and put everything in the fridge for 60 mins.
- Enjoy.

Amount per serving (4 total)

Timing Information:

Preparation	
Cooking	20 m
Total Time	1 h 20 m

Nutritional Information:

Calories	155 kcal
Fat	7.9 g
Carbohydrates	19.4g
Protein	4 g
Cholesterol	0 mg
Sodium	248 mg

* Percent Daily Values are based on a 2,000 calorie diet.

HONEY AVOCADO AND APPLES

Ingredients

- 2 avocado, peeled, pitted and diced
- 1 large red apple, cored and diced
- 2 tbsps honey
- 1/2 C. raisins, soaked in water and drained
- 1 tbsp hulled sunflower seeds

Directions

- Get a bowl, combine: raisins, apples, and avocados.
- Stir the mix to distribute the raisins then top everything with the sunflower seeds and the honey.
- Enjoy.

Amount per serving (4 total)

Timing Information:

Preparation	
Cooking	10 m
Total Time	10 m

Nutritional Information:

Calories	294 kcal
Fat	15.9 g
Carbohydrates	41.4g
Protein	3.2 g
Cholesterol	0 mg
Sodium	10 mg

* Percent Daily Values are based on a 2,000 calorie diet.

CALIFORNIA STYLE TACOS

Ingredients

- 1 lb ground turkey
- 1/2 sweet onion, chopped
- salt and ground black pepper to taste
- 1 pinch garlic powder, or to taste
- 8 taco shells, warmed
- 2 avocados, peeled and mashed
- 3/4 C. reduced-fat sour cream
- 1 C. pico de gallo
- 1 C. shredded Colby cheese

Directions

- Stir fry your onions and turkey until the turkey is fully done then add in the garlic powder, some pepper, and some salt.

- Remove any excess oils then coat your taco shells with sour cream and avocado.
- Evenly divide your Pico de Gallo, Colby, and turkey between the shells and serve your tacos.
- Enjoy.

Amount per serving (4 total)

Timing Information:

Preparation	10 m
Cooking	15 m
Total Time	25 m

Nutritional Information:

Calories	738 kcal
Fat	48.2 g
Carbohydrates	43.2g
Protein	37.8 g
Cholesterol	133 mg
Sodium	841 mg

* Percent Daily Values are based on a 2,000 calorie diet.

Avocado Wraps with Colby Jack

Ingredients

- 1 (4 oz.) package cream cheese, softened
- 1 tsp ground cumin
- 1 clove garlic, diced
- 1/8 tsp dried red pepper flakes
- 6 tomato and oregano tortillas
- 6 lettuce leaves, rinsed and dried
- 12 slices deli sliced roast beef
- 1 avocado, cubed
- 1 tomato, seeded and chopped
- 1 C. shredded Colby-Monterey Jack cheese

Directions

- Get a bowl, combine: chili flakes, cream cheese, garlic, and cumin.

- Coat each tortilla with cream cheese equally then lay a piece of lettuce on each.
- Now layer your cheese, 2 pieces of beef, tomatoes, and avocado on each.
- Shape the tortilla into a burrito and cut each one in half.
- Enjoy.

Amount per serving (6 total)

Timing Information:

Preparation	
Cooking	20 m
Total Time	20 m

Nutritional Information:

Calories	533 kcal
Fat	26.6 g
Carbohydrates	48.4g
Protein	26.1 g
Cholesterol	70 mg
Sodium	1388 mg

* Percent Daily Values are based on a 2,000 calorie diet.

Avocado and Beef

Ingredients

- 2 C. water
- 1 C. uncooked long-grain white rice
- 1 (16 oz.) can refried beans
- salt to taste
- garlic powder to taste
- 1 tbsp olive oil
- 2 small onions, chopped
- 4 beef steaks
- 2 avocados, peeled, pitted and sliced

Directions

- Get your grill hot and coat the grate with oil.
- Get some water boiling in a large pot then add in the rice.
- Get the mix boiling again then place lid on the pot.

- Now set the heat to low, and let the rice cook for 22 mins.
- Begin to stir fry your onions until they are soft and brown.
- Now grill your meat for 9 mins each side or until it reaches your preferred level of doneness.
- Coat the meat first with the refried beans then lay your avocado over the beans and finally the fried onions.
- Enjoy over the rice.

Amount per serving (4 total)

Timing Information:

Preparation	35 m
Cooking	10 m
Total Time	45 m

Nutritional Information:

Calories	801 kcal
Fat	32.3 g
Carbohydrates	66.2g
Protein	60.7 g
Cholesterol	1143 mg
Sodium	480 mg

* Percent Daily Values are based on a 2,000 calorie diet.

AVOCADO DRESSING II

Ingredients

- 1 avocado, peeled and pitted
- 1 C. mayonnaise
- 5 anchovy filets, rinsed and chopped
- 2 tbsps chopped green onion
- 1 tbsp lemon juice
- 1 clove garlic, chopped
- salt and pepper to taste

Directions

- Add the following to the bowl of a blender: pepper, avocado, garlic, mayo, salt, anchovies, lemon juice, and green onions.
- Blend the mix until it is smooth then place everything into a container for storage.

- Place a lid on the container or cover it with plastic.
- Place everything in the fridge for 1 day.
- Enjoy.

Amount per serving (6 total)

Timing Information:

Preparation	
Cooking	15 m
Total Time	1 d 15 m

Nutritional Information:

Calories	326 kcal
Fat	34.4 g
Carbohydrates	4.5g
Protein	2 g
Cholesterol	17 mg
Sodium	333 mg

* Percent Daily Values are based on a 2,000 calorie diet.

Easy Avocado Mousse

Ingredients

- 1 1/4 C. fat-free sour cream
- 3 tbsps low-fat creamy salad dressing
- 1 tsp sweet pickle relish
- 2 tsps yellow mustard
- 1/8 tsp dried diced onion
- 2 (5 oz.) cans tuna in water, drained
- 2 avocados, cut into 1/4-inch dice

Directions

- Get a bowl, combine: onion flakes, sour cream, mustard, dressing, and relish.
- Stir the mix until it is even and smooth then add in your tuna and stir the fish into the mix.

- Now gradually add in your avocado and combine everything but try not to mash it.
- Place a covering of plastic on the bowl and put everything in fridge until it is cold.
- Enjoy.

Amount per serving (4 total)

Timing Information:

Preparation	
Cooking	15 m
Total Time	45 m

Nutritional Information:

Calories	345 kcal
Fat	17.6 g
Carbohydrates	24.2g
Protein	23.6 g
Cholesterol	35 mg
Sodium	243 mg

* Percent Daily Values are based on a 2,000 calorie diet.

Avocado Lunch

Ingredients

- 4 slices bacon
- 1 (6 oz.) can solid white tuna packed in water
- 1/2 tsp Dijon mustard
- 1/2 tsp prepared horseradish
- 1 tbsp sweet pickle relish
- 1 tbsp diced red onion
- 1/4 tsp paprika
- black pepper to taste
- 2 hoagie buns, split
- 1 avocado, peeled, pitted and sliced
- 1 tomato, sliced
- 2 slices provolone cheese
- 2 lettuce leaves

Directions

- Microwave your bacon for 5 mins.
- At the same time get a bowl, combine: the red onion, tuna, relish, Dijon, and horseradish.
- Stir the mix to evenly distribute everything amongst the fish then add in your pepper and paprika.
- Combine the spices into the tuna then equally top your rolls with it to form sandwiches.
- Before serving the sandwiches layer half of the tomato and half of the avocado on each one.
- Then place a piece of cheese, a piece of lettuce, and 2 pieces of bacon on each sandwich.
- Enjoy.

Amount per serving (2 total)

Timing Information:

Preparation	6 m
Cooking	4 m
Total Time	10 m

Nutritional Information:

Calories	872 kcal
Fat	37.8 g
Carbohydrates	84g
Protein	49.9 g
Cholesterol	165 mg
Sodium	1583 mg

* Percent Daily Values are based on a 2,000 calorie diet.

Avocado White Sauce

Ingredients

- 1 large avocado, peeled and pitted
- 2 cloves garlic, diced
- 1 lemons, juiced
- 1/4 C. sour cream
- 1/2 C. chopped seeded cucumber
- 1/2 tsp red pepper flakes, or to taste
- 1 tbsp chopped fresh cilantro
- 1 tbsp chopped fresh mint
- salt and pepper to taste

Directions

- Get a bowl, combine: cucumber, avocado, sour cream, lemon juice, and garlic.

- Mash the mix together then add in your pepper, pepper flakes, salt, mint, and cilantro.
- Stir the spices in then place a covering of plastic on the bowl and put everything in the fridge for 60 mins.
- Enjoy.

Amount per serving (8 total)

Timing Information:

Preparation	
Cooking	5 m
Total Time	5 m

Nutritional Information:

Calories	78 kcal
Fat	6.8 g
Carbohydrates	5.5g
Protein	1.2 g
Cholesterol	3 mg
Sodium	7 mg

* Percent Daily Values are based on a 2,000 calorie diet.

CRAB AND AVOCADOS

Ingredients

- 1 avocado, peeled, pitted, and sliced
- 1 hard-boiled egg
- 1/3 C. flaked cooked crabmeat
- 1 tsp mustard
- 1 tbsp mayonnaise
- 1/4 tsp lemon pepper seasoning
- 1/4 tsp garlic salt
- 1/4 tsp cayenne pepper
- 1/8 tsp curry powder

Directions

- Get a bowl, mash: egg and avocado.
- Now combine in: mustard, mayo, and crab.

- Stir the mix until it is combined nicely then add in: the curry powder, lemon pepper mix, cayenne, and garlic salt.
- Combine the spices in evenly then serve.
- Enjoy.

Amount per serving (2 total)

Timing Information:

Preparation	
Cooking	10 m
Total Time	10 m

Nutritional Information:

Calories	277 kcal
Fat	23.3 g
Carbohydrates	9.7g
Protein	10.4 g
Cholesterol	126 mg
Sodium	476 mg

* Percent Daily Values are based on a 2,000 calorie diet.

Avocado and Chive Roast

Ingredients

- 1 avocado, halved and pitted
- 2 eggs
- salt and ground black pepper to taste
- 1 pinch cayenne pepper
- 1/4 C. crumbled cooked bacon
- 1 tbsp chopped fresh chives

Directions

- Set your oven to 425 degrees before doing anything else.
- Layer half the pieces of avocado into ramekins then break an egg into each one.
- Top the mix with some cayenne, black pepper, and salt. Then layer everything in a jellyroll pan.

- Cook the contents in the oven for 17 mins then top each one with some chives and bacon.
- Enjoy.

Amount per serving (2 total)

Timing Information:

Preparation	10 m
Cooking	15 m
Total Time	25 m

Nutritional Information:

Calories	355 kcal
Fat	29.1 g
Carbohydrates	9.4g
Protein	16.7 g
Cholesterol	211 mg
Sodium	674 mg

* Percent Daily Values are based on a 2,000 calorie diet.

Avocado Chili

Ingredients

- 5 fresh tomatillos, husks removed
- 4 serrano chile peppers, or to taste
- 2 tbsps chopped fresh cilantro
- 1 ripe avocado, peeled, pitted, and quartered
- salt to taste

Directions

- Place the following in the bowl of a food processor: cilantro, tomatillos, and serrano's.
- Pulse the mix until it is smooth then combine in a quarter of the avocado.
- Continue blending the avocadoes in quarters until all of it has combined then top the entire mix with some salt and pulse the spice into the mix a few more times.

- Enjoy.

Amount per serving (6 total)

Timing Information:

Preparation	
Cooking	10 m
Total Time	10 m

Nutritional Information:

Calories	64 kcal
Fat	5.2 g
Carbohydrates	4.8g
Protein	1 g
Cholesterol	0 mg
Sodium	3 mg

* Percent Daily Values are based on a 2,000 calorie diet.

South of the Border Avocado

Ingredients

- 3 (6 oz.) cans canned chicken, drained
- 1 tbsp cilantro, finely chopped
- 1/2 tsp chili powder, or more to taste
- 3 avocados, halved lengthwise and pitted
- 1 tsp lime juice, or to taste

Directions

- Get a bowl, combine: chili powder, cilantro, and chicken.
- Lay out your pieces of avocado on a dish for serving then top them with the lime juice.
- Evenly divide your cilantro mix between the avocado pieces.
- Enjoy.

Amount per serving (3 total)

Timing Information:

Preparation	
Cooking	10 m
Total Time	10 m

Nutritional Information:

Calories	601 kcal
Fat	42.9 g
Carbohydrates	17.6g
Protein	40.7 g
Cholesterol	104 mg
Sodium	864 mg

* Percent Daily Values are based on a 2,000 calorie diet.

Avocado Dip

Ingredients

- 1 avocado, peeled, pitted, and mashed
- 1/2 onion, diced
- 1/2 C. chopped cooked chicken
- 1 tbsp lime juice
- 1/4 tsp garlic powder
- salt and ground black pepper to taste

Directions

- Get a bowl, combine: pepper, avocado, salt, onion, garlic powder, chicken, and lime juice.
- Enjoy.

Amount per serving (6 total)

Timing Information:

Preparation	
Cooking	15 m
Total Time	15 m

Nutritional Information:

Calories	84 kcal
Fat	5.8 g
Carbohydrates	4.9g
Protein	4.1 g
Cholesterol	9 mg
Sodium	10 mg

* Percent Daily Values are based on a 2,000 calorie diet.

Countryside Avocado Bake

Ingredients

- 7 tbsps butter, divided
- 1 tbsp olive oil
- 8 skinless, boneless chicken breast halves
- 1/4 C. all-purpose flour
- 1 C. light cream
- 1 C. chicken broth
- 3/4 tsp Morton(R) Kosher Salt
- 1/4 tsp ground black pepper
- 1/2 C. grated Parmesan cheese
- 2 dashes hot pepper sauce
- 1/2 tsp dried rosemary, crushed
- 1/2 tsp dried basil
- 3 C. sliced fresh mushrooms
- 1/4 C. sherry
- 1/2 C. sliced almonds, toasted

- 2 avocados

Directions

- Set your oven to 350 degrees before doing anything else.
- Begin to fry your chicken in olive oil and butter until it is fully done and browned.
- Then layer the pieces of chicken in a casserole dish.
- Add in 4 more tbsps of butter to the pan then add in the flour.
- Stir and heat the mix for 4 mins then gradually add in your broth and cream.
- Stir the mix and let it get thick.
- Add in: the herbs, kosher salt, hot sauce, black pepper, and parmesan.
- Once the mix is thick shut the heat.
- Now stir fry your mushrooms in 2 more tbsp of butter in a separate pan then add in the sherry and let everything simmer until all the sherry has reduced a bit.

- Now top the chicken with mushrooms and pour the cream sauce over everything.
- Cook the chicken in the oven for 30 mins then top it with almonds and continue cooking for 6 more mins.
- Now remove the skin form your avocado and slice it.
- Top the chicken with the avocado pieces.
- Enjoy.

Amount per serving (8 total)

Timing Information:

Preparation	25 m
Cooking	35 m
Total Time	1 h

Nutritional Information:

Calories	458 kcal
Fat	30.2 g
Carbohydrates	13.1g
Protein	34.7 g
Cholesterol	111 mg
Sodium	589 mg

* Percent Daily Values are based on a 2,000 calorie diet.

Buffalo Avocado Sandwich

Ingredients

- cooking spray
- 2 flour tortillas
- 1 C. grated Cheddar cheese
- 1 small tomato, seeded and diced
- 1/2 C. onion, diced
- 3 slices cooked bacon, crumbled, or more to taste
- salt and ground black pepper to taste
- 1 avocado, peeled, pitted, and sliced
- 1 tbsp chopped fresh cilantro
- 1 tsp ranch dressing
- 1 tsp buffalo ranch dressing

Directions

- Coat a frying pan with nonstick spray then set your oven to 375 degrees before doing anything else.
- Begin to toast your tortilla for 60 secs in the frying pan then layer half of the following on it: cheddar, tomato, onion, and bacon.
- Top the layers with some pepper and salt. Then let the contents heat for 60 more secs until the cheese is melted.
- Place the pan in the oven for 2 mins then place more pepper, salt, the cilantro, and half of avocado pieces.
- Top the tortilla with some of the ranch and buffalo ranch then shape everything into a burrito.
- Continue forming burritos in this manner until all the ingredients have been used up.
- Enjoy.

Amount per serving (2 total)

Timing Information:

Preparation	15 m
Cooking	10 m
Total Time	25 m

Nutritional Information:

Calories	648 kcal
Fat	43.6 g
Carbohydrates	42.6g
Protein	24.6 g
Cholesterol	71 mg
Sodium	930 mg

* Percent Daily Values are based on a 2,000 calorie diet.

Avocado Pizza

Ingredients

- 2 avocados, peeled, pitted and diced
- 1 tbsp chopped fresh cilantro
- 1 tbsp fresh lime juice, or to taste
- salt to taste
- 1 clove garlic, peeled
- 4 (7 inch) pre-baked pizza crusts
- 1 tbsp olive oil
- 1 C. chopped cooked chicken breast meat
- 1 C. cherry tomatoes, quartered
- 1 C. shredded Monterey Jack cheese
- 1 pinch cayenne pepper

Directions

- Get your oven's broiler hot.

- Now puree the following in a food processor until it is smooth: cilantro and avocado.
- Slowly add in your lime juice and continue to pulse the mix.
- Cut your pieces of garlic in half then rub the cut portions of the garlic on the crusts.
- Now coat the crusts with olive oil then layer your puree over the crust like a sauce.
- Place your tomatoes and chicken evenly over the crusts then top everything with cayenne and cheese.
- Place your crusts on some pizza dishes or on a cookie sheet and cook them in the oven for 7 mins.
- Enjoy.

Amount per serving (4 total)

Timing Information:

Preparation	20 m
Cooking	5 m
Total Time	25 m

Nutritional Information:

Calories	798 kcal
Fat	38 g
Carbohydrates	82.4g
Protein	38.9 g
Cholesterol	66 mg
Sodium	1011 mg

* Percent Daily Values are based on a 2,000 calorie diet.

MARIA'S GAZPACHO

Ingredients

- 2 1/2 C. tomato-vegetable juice cocktail
- 2 1/2 C. vegetable broth
- 3 large tomatoes, diced
- 3 large avocados, peeled, pitted, and cut into bite-sized pieces
- 1 C. diced cucumber
- 1 (8 oz.) can chopped tomatoes with juice
- 1/2 C. chopped green bell pepper
- 1/2 C. chopped red bell pepper
- 1/4 C. extra-virgin olive oil
- 3 green onions, thinly sliced
- 1 lemon, juiced, or more to taste
- 2 tbsps diced fresh cilantro
- 2 tbsps white wine vinegar
- 1 dash hot pepper sauce

- salt and ground black pepper to taste

Directions

- Get a bowl, combine: black pepper, tomato-veggie juice, salt, veggie broth, hot sauce, tomatoes, canned tomatoes and their liquid, vinegar, bell peppers, cilantro, olive oil, cucumbers, avocados, lemon juice, and green onions.
- Place a covering of plastic on the bowl and put everything in the fridge for 4 hrs.
- Enjoy.

Amount per serving (8 total)

Timing Information:

Preparation	
Cooking	30 m
Total Time	3 h 30 m

Nutritional Information:

Calories	287 kcal
Fat	23.1 g
Carbohydrates	21g
Protein	4.5 g
Cholesterol	0 mg
Sodium	392 mg

* Percent Daily Values are based on a 2,000 calorie diet.

Avocado Drink

Ingredients

- 2 avocados, skins removed, pitted, chunked
- 1 tbsp orange zest
- 1/8 tsp ground ginger
- 1 tsp salt
- 1 pinch ground black pepper
- 3 C. milk

Directions

- Add the following to the bowl of a blender: pepper, orange peel, ginger salt, and avocado chunks.
- Pulse the mix until it is smooth then add in your milk slowly while continuing to blend.
- Keep blending the mix until it is smooth. Then place everything in a serving container.

- Place a lid or some plastic on the container and put everything in the fridge until it is cold.
- Enjoy.

Amount per serving (5 total)

Timing Information:

Preparation	10 m
Cooking	10 m
Total Time	20 m

Nutritional Information:

Calories	204 kcal
Fat	14.7 g
Carbohydrates	14.2g
Protein	6.5 g
Cholesterol	12 mg
Sodium	531 mg

* Percent Daily Values are based on a 2,000 calorie diet.

CREAMY AVOCADO STEW

Ingredients

- 2 avocado, peeled, pitted and diced
- 1 tbsp chopped shallots
- 1 tbsp olive oil
- 2 C. chicken stock
- 1 C. heavy cream
- salt and pepper to taste
- 1/4 tsp ground nutmeg
- 1 tomato, peeled, seeded and diced

Directions

- Add your avocado to the bowl of a food processor and begin to puree it.
- Begin to stir fry your shallots in olive oil until they are soft then shut the heat.

- Get a bowl, combine: chicken stock, shallots, cream, and avocado.
- Stir the mix until it is smooth then add in the nutmeg, some pepper and salt.
- Place a covering of plastic on the bowl and put the mix in the fridge for 30 mins.
- When serving the dish top the soup with your tomatoes.
- Enjoy.

Amount per serving (4 total)

Timing Information:

Preparation	15 m
Cooking	10 m
Total Time	55 m

Nutritional Information:

Calories	410 kcal
Fat	40.6 g
Carbohydrates	12.5g
Protein	3.9 g
Cholesterol	82 mg
Sodium	374 mg

* Percent Daily Values are based on a 2,000 calorie diet.

SUMMERTIME AVOCADOS

Ingredients

- 1/4 C. olive oil, or as needed
- 1 pinch ground chipotle pepper, or more to taste
- 1 pinch chili powder, or more to taste
- 4 avocados, halved and pitted

Directions

- Get your outdoor grill hot and coat the grate with oil.
- Get a bowl, combine: chili powder, olive oil, and chipotle.
- Stir the mix until it is smooth then top the avocado flesh with it.
- Cook the avocados for 6 mins on the grill with the insides directly on the grate.
- Enjoy.

Amount per serving (8 total)

Timing Information:

Preparation	10 m
Cooking	5 m
Total Time	15 m

Nutritional Information:

Calories	221 kcal
Fat	21.5 g
Carbohydrates	8.6g
Protein	2 g
Cholesterol	0 mg
Sodium	8 mg

* Percent Daily Values are based on a 2,000 calorie diet.

STUFFED AVOCADOS

Ingredients

- 1/2 C. flaked cooked crabmeat
- 1/2 C. cooked small shrimp
- 2 tbsps peeled and diced cucumber
- 1 tbsp mayonnaise
- 1 tsp chopped fresh parsley
- 1 pinch salt
- 1 pinch ground black pepper
- 1 pinch paprika
- 1 avocado

Directions

- Get a bowl, combine: parsley, crab, mayo, cucumber, and shrimp.

- Stir the mix until it is smooth then add in the pepper and salt.
- Place a covering of plastic on the bowl and put everything in the fridge until it is cold.
- Now take out the flesh of the avocado and save it for another recipe (like a dressing) then add the seafood mix into the shells.
- Top everything with some paprika.
- Enjoy.

Amount per serving (2 total)

Timing Information:

Preparation	
Cooking	15 m
Total Time	15 m

Nutritional Information:

Calories	283 kcal
Fat	21.1 g
Carbohydrates	10g
Protein	16.5 g
Cholesterol	91 mg
Sodium	246 mg

* Percent Daily Values are based on a 2,000 calorie diet.

Rustic Avocados

Ingredients

- 2 Haas avocados, peeled, pitted, and sliced
- 1 tbsp butter
- 1/2 C. slivered almonds, finely chopped
- sea salt to taste

Directions

- Toast your almonds in the butter once it has melted for 3 mins then lay your pieces of avocado on a serving dish.
- Top the avocados with the almonds and the salt as well.
- Enjoy.

Amount per serving (4 total)

Timing Information:

Preparation	10 m
Cooking	5 m
Total Time	20 m

Nutritional Information:

Calories	268 kcal
Fat	24.5 g
Carbohydrates	11.2g
Protein	4.9 g
Cholesterol	8 mg
Sodium	109 mg

* Percent Daily Values are based on a 2,000 calorie diet.

Avocado Appetizer

Ingredients

- 3 avocados, halved and pitted
- 2 hard-boiled eggs, peeled
- 1/2 onion, diced
- 1 1/2 tsps diced garlic
- 1/2 tsp lime juice
- 1/2 tsp smoked paprika
- 1/4 tsp cayenne pepper
- salt and ground black pepper to taste

Directions

- Remove the flesh of the avocado into a bowl but keep the skin.
- Add your eggs to the avocado and mash everything together.

- Now add in the black pepper, onion, salt, garlic, cayenne, lime juice, and paprika.
- Evenly divide the mix between the avocado shells then serve.
- Enjoy.

Amount per serving (6 total)

Timing Information:

Preparation	
Cooking	15 m
Total Time	15 m

Nutritional Information:

Calories	196 kcal
Fat	16.6 g
Carbohydrates	10.9g
Protein	4.4 g
Cholesterol	71 mg
Sodium	29 mg

* Percent Daily Values are based on a 2,000 calorie diet.

Southern Avocado

Ingredients

- 2 C. vegetable oil (for frying)
- 1 C. all-purpose flour
- 2 tbsps salt-free herb seasoning blend
- 1 pinch ground cumin
- 1 avocado, peeled, pitted and sliced
- 1 egg, beaten

Directions

- Get your oil hot to 365 degrees before doing anything else.
- Get a bowl, combine: cumin, herb spice, and flour.
- Get a 2nd bowl and add in the whisked eggs.
- Coat your avocado first with the eggs then with the cumin mix.

- For 2 mins fry the avocado in oil then flip it and continue frying everything for 2 more mins.
- Place the avocado on some paper towel then serve.
- Enjoy.

Amount per serving (2 total)

Timing Information:

Preparation	15 m
Cooking	5 m
Total Time	20 m

Nutritional Information:

Calories	620 kcal
Fat	39.9 g
Carbohydrates	56.7g
Protein	11.7 g
Cholesterol	93 mg
Sodium	44 mg

* Percent Daily Values are based on a 2,000 calorie diet.

Catalina's Ceviche

Ingredients

- 2 lbs tilapia fillets, cut into cubes, or more to taste
- 2 small semi-firm avocados, cut into cubes, or more to taste
- 8 cloves garlic, diced, or more to taste
- 1 habanero pepper, diced
- 2 tsps chopped fresh cilantro
- 1 tsp salt
- 1/2 tsp ground black pepper
- 1/8 tsp ground ginger
- 30 fluid oz. lime juice, or as needed
- 1/2 large red onion, finely chopped
- 20 small flour tortillas

Directions

- Get a bowl, combine: ginger, tilapia, pepper, avocados, salt, garlic, cilantro, and habanero.
- Submerge the fish in the lime juice and layer your onions on top.
- Place a covering of plastic on the bowl and place everything in the fridge for 5 hours.
- Evenly divide the mix amongst your tortillas.
- Enjoy.

Amount per serving (20 total)

Timing Information:

Preparation	
Cooking	20 m
Total Time	5 h 20 m

Nutritional Information:

Calories	188 kcal
Fat	5.6 g
Carbohydrates	22.6g
Protein	12.6 g
Cholesterol	17 mg
Sodium	343 mg

* Percent Daily Values are based on a 2,000 calorie diet.

Macaroni and Avocados

Ingredients

- 1 lb elbow macaroni
- 1 1/2 C. skim milk
- 3 small garlic cloves
- 1/4 tsp ground nutmeg
- 1/4 tsp chili powder
- 1 C. flat-leaf parsley leaves
- 2 Avocados, halved, pitted, peeled and diced, divided
- 5 oz. Cheddar cheese, cubed
- 1 tbsp lime juice
- 1/2 C. chopped chives

Directions

- Get your pasta boiling in water and salt for 9 mins then remove all the liquids.

- At the same time, get the following boiling in a separate pan: chili powder, milk, nutmeg, and garlic.
- Once the mix is boiling, set the heat to low, and let the mix gently cook for 7 mins.
- Begin to puree the following with a food processor: hot milk with garlic, parsley, lime juice, 1.5 C. avocado, and the cheeses.
- Once the mix is smooth top the pasta with it and garnish everything with 1/2 more of diced avocado, and chives.
- Enjoy.

Amount per serving (6 total)

Timing Information:

Preparation	
Cooking	15 m
Total Time	15 m

Nutritional Information:

Calories	458 kcal
Fat	12.8 g
Carbohydrates	67.3g
Protein	19.6 g
Cholesterol	6 mg
Sodium	187 mg

* Percent Daily Values are based on a 2,000 calorie diet.

Avocado Bisque

Ingredients

- 3 avocados
- 1 (14.5 oz.) can chicken broth
- 2 C. milk
- 1 tsp lemon juice
- 2 tsps diced onion
- 1/2 lb cooked fresh shrimp
- 1/8 tsp salt
- 1/8 tsp ground black pepper

Directions

- Get the following simmering while stirring: chopped onion, avocado, lemon juice, lemon juice, milk, and broth.
- Once the mix is simmering add in the pepper, salt, and shrimp.

- Now shut the heat and serve the dish.
- Enjoy.

Amount per serving (12 total)

Timing Information:

Preparation	10 m
Cooking	10 m
Total Time	20 m

Nutritional Information:

Calories	124 kcal
Fat	8.5 g
Carbohydrates	6.3g
Protein	7.1 g
Cholesterol	42 mg
Sodium	98 mg

* Percent Daily Values are based on a 2,000 calorie diet.

Avocado Chili II

Ingredients

- 1 (8 oz.) package uncooked spaghetti
- 1 avocado, pitted, peeled, and cubed
- 1 tbsp lime juice
- 1 (15 oz.) can vegetarian chili
- 1/3 C. sliced green onion
- 2 large tomatoes, diced
- 1 tsp diced garlic
- 1/3 C. chopped fresh cilantro

Directions

- Boil your pasta in water and salt for 9 mins then remove all the liquids.
- Get a bowl, combine: lime juice, and avocado.

- Get a 2nd bowl, combine: cilantro, chili, garlic, tomatoes, and green onions.
- Place your pasta on a serving plate then top each serving with an equal amount of the avocadoes then the tomato mix.
- Enjoy.

Amount per serving (6 total)

Timing Information:

Preparation	10 m
Cooking	10 m
Total Time	20 m

Nutritional Information:

Calories	210 kcal
Fat	5.6 g
Carbohydrates	34.5g
Protein	6.5 g
Cholesterol	0 mg
Sodium	16 mg

* Percent Daily Values are based on a 2,000 calorie diet.

Avocado Lemon Dessert

Ingredients

- 1 avocado, mashed
- 1 (14 oz.) can sweetened condensed milk
- 1/4 C. fresh lemon juice, or to taste
- 1 (9 inch) pie shell, baked

Directions

- Get a bowl, combine your mashed avocado and milk.
- Then add in the lemon juice and combine it in evenly.
- Place everything into the crust.
- Place a covering of plastic over everything and put the pie in the fridge for 5 hrs.
- Top the pie with some whipped topping before serving.
- Enjoy.

Amount per serving (8 total)

Timing Information:

Preparation	
Cooking	10 m
Total Time	10 m

Nutritional Information:

Calories	280 kcal
Fat	13.1 g
Carbohydrates	37.3g
Protein	5.1 g
Cholesterol	17 mg
Sodium	166 mg

* Percent Daily Values are based on a 2,000 calorie diet.

PEPPER JACK AVOCADOS

Ingredients

- 2 tbsps butter
- 1 tbsp sesame oil
- 1 pinch garlic powder, or to taste
- salt and ground black pepper to taste
- 5 oz. frozen cooked small shrimp
- 1/3 C. unsalted roasted cashews
- 2 tbsps chopped green chilies
- 1 low-carbohydrate tortilla, halved
- 1 avocado, peeled, pitted, and sliced
- 2 oz. shredded pepper jack cheese
- 2 oz. shredded Cheddar cheese

Directions

- Begin to get your butter melting in a frying pan with the sesame oil then add in the pepper, salt, and garlic power.
- Stir the spices into the butter then add in your chili pepper, cashews, and shrimp.
- Fry the mix for 7 mins.
- Now place your pieces of tortilla in a casserole dish and layer half of the avocado pieces on each.
- Top the avocado with half of the shrimp mix then coat everything with the butter from the pan.
- Add half of the cheddar and pepper jack to each. Then place the tortillas under the broiler for 6 mins.
- Enjoy.

Amount per serving (2 total)

Timing Information:

Preparation	15 m
Cooking	10 m
Total Time	25 m

Nutritional Information:

Calories	777 kcal
Fat	63.9 g
Carbohydrates	23.7g
Protein	36.1 g
Cholesterol	227 mg
Sodium	930 mg

* Percent Daily Values are based on a 2,000 calorie diet.

AVOCADO COCONUT PUDDING

Ingredients

- 2 avocados, peeled, pitted, and diced
- 3/4 C. sweetened cream of coconut
- 5 tbsps cocoa powder
- 1/2 tsp ground cinnamon
- 1/4 tsp cayenne pepper

Directions

- Add the following to the bowl of a blender and process the mix until it is pudding like: cayenne, avocados, cinnamon, coconut, and cocoa.
- Pour everything into a bowl and place a covering of plastic on the bowl. Place the mix in the fridge for 3 hrs.
- Enjoy.

Amount per serving (6 total)

Timing Information:

Preparation	
Cooking	10 m
Total Time	3 h 10 m

Nutritional Information:

Calories	261 kcal
Fat	17 g
Carbohydrates	30.6g
Protein	2.2 g
Cholesterol	0 mg
Sodium	25 mg

* Percent Daily Values are based on a 2,000 calorie diet.

Avocado Cheesecake

Ingredients

- 1 1/2 C. heavy whipping cream
- 3/4 C. white sugar
- 1 1/2 ripe avocados, peeled and pitted
- 2 (3 oz.) packages cream cheese, softened
- 1/2 C. fresh lime juice
- 1 (8 inch) prepared graham cracker crust

Directions

- Get your cream simmering in a pan then shut the heat and add in the sugar. Stir the mix until the sugar is fully incorporated then pour everything into a bowl.
- Add your cream cheese and avocado to the bowl of a food processor and pulse the mix until it is smooth.

- Combine in the lime juice and continue processing the mix.
- Place the mix into an ice cream maker and freeze it in line with the associated instructions on the ice cream maker.
- Now add the mix to the crust once it is done then place it all in the freezer for 3 hrs.
- Place the pie on the countertop and let it sit for 20 mins.
- Enjoy.

Amount per serving (8 total)

Timing Information:

Preparation	20 m
Cooking	5 m
Total Time	3 h 35 m

Nutritional Information:

Calories	470 kcal
Fat	34.8 g
Carbohydrates	39g
Protein	4.2 g
Cholesterol	85 mg
Sodium	204 mg

* Percent Daily Values are based on a 2,000 calorie diet.

Avocado Bars

Ingredients

- 2 C. all-purpose flour
- 1/2 C. white sugar
- 2 tbsps diced fresh rosemary
- 2 limes, zested and juiced
- 1/2 C. butter
- 1 1/2 C. white sugar
- 4 eggs
- 1 avocado, peeled, pitted, and mashed

Directions

- Coat a casserole dish with oil then set your oven to 350 degrees before doing anything else.
- Get a bowl, combine: the lime zest, flour, rosemary, and half C. of sugar.

- Now use a pastry cutter to add in your butter in small pieces.
- Place one C. of the flour to the side. Then layer the rest in the bottom of the casserole dish.
- Cook everything in the oven for 12 mins.
- Get a bowl, combine: mashed avocado, half of the reserve flour, eggs, 1.5 C. sugar, and lime juice.
- Layer the mix over the contents in the casserole dish and add the rest of the reserved flour mix.
- Continue cooking everything in the oven for 27 more mins. Then slice everything into about 40 bars.
- Place a covering of plastic on the dish and put everything in fridge until cold.
- Enjoy.

Amount per serving (48 total)

Timing Information:

Preparation	10 m
Cooking	30 m
Total Time	40 m

Nutritional Information:

Calories	82 kcal
Fat	3 g
Carbohydrates	13g
Protein	1.2 g
Cholesterol	21 mg
Sodium	20 mg

* Percent Daily Values are based on a 2,000 calorie diet.

THE AVOCADO SANDWICH

Ingredients

- 1/3 C. egg-free mayonnaise
- 2 large green onions, sliced
- 2 tbsps prepared yellow mustard
- 1/4 tsp ground black pepper
- 1/4 tsp paprika
- 2 large semi-firm avocados, diced
- 1/2 tsp kala namak (black salt)
- 8 slices potato bread

Directions

- Get a bowl, combine: paprika, mayo, black pepper, green onions, and mustard.
- Stir the mix until it is smooth then add in some black salt and the avocado pieces.

- Equally top four pieces of bread with the mix then form sandwiches with other pieces.
- Enjoy.

Amount per serving (4 total)

Timing Information:

Preparation	
Cooking	15 m
Total Time	15 m

Nutritional Information:

Calories	466 kcal
Fat	32 g
Carbohydrates	42.3g
Protein	7.7 g
Cholesterol	1 mg
Sodium	736 mg

* Percent Daily Values are based on a 2,000 calorie diet.

CABBAGE AND AVOCADOS

Ingredients

- 3 C. shredded red cabbage
- 3 C. shredded green cabbage
- 2 avocado, peeled, pitted, and diced
- 1/4 C. sesame seeds
- 3 tbsps chopped red onion
- 3 tbsps chopped cilantro leaves
- 2 tbsps lime juice

Directions

- Get a bowl, combine: lime juice, red cabbage, cilantro, green cabbage, red onions, sesame seeds, and avocado.
- Enjoy.

Amount per serving (2 total)

Timing Information:

Preparation	
Cooking	10 m
Total Time	10 m

Nutritional Information:

Calories	488 kcal
Fat	38.7 g
Carbohydrates	36.4g
Protein	10.2 g
Cholesterol	0 mg
Sodium	57 mg

* Percent Daily Values are based on a 2,000 calorie diet.

MEDITERRANEAN AVOCADOS

Ingredients

- 2 avocados, peeled, pitted and diced
- 2 tomatoes, diced
- 2 (2 oz.) cans chopped black olives
- 2 (4 oz.) cans diced green chilies
- 1 lemon, juiced
- salt and pepper to taste

Directions

- Get a bowl, combine: chilies, avocados, olives, and tomatoes.
- Stir the mix until it is smooth then coat the mix with some freshly squeezed lemon juice.
- Now top everything with some pepper and salt.
- Enjoy.

Amount per serving (6 total)

Timing Information:

Preparation	
Cooking	5 m
Total Time	5 m

Nutritional Information:

Calories	146 kcal
Fat	11.9 g
Carbohydrates	11.2g
Protein	2.2 g
Cholesterol	0 mg
Sodium	607 mg

* Percent Daily Values are based on a 2,000 calorie diet.

CURRY AVOCADO SALAD DRESSING III

Ingredients

- 1 large ripe avocado, peeled and diced
- 1 (8 oz.) container sour cream
- 1 (1 oz.) package French onion soup mix
- 2 cloves garlic, diced
- 1 tbsp curry powder
- 1 lemon, juiced

Directions

- With a high speed blend the following: lemon juice, avocado, curry powder, sour cream, garlic, and soup mix.
- Continue blending the mix until it is smooth then place everything into a mason jar.
- Tightly seal the jar and place everything in the fridge until it is cold.

- Enjoy.

Amount per serving (8 total)

Timing Information:

Preparation	
Cooking	15 m
Total Time	15 m

Nutritional Information:

Calories	115 kcal
Fat	9.8 g
Carbohydrates	6.7g
Protein	1.8 g
Cholesterol	12 mg
Sodium	327 mg

* Percent Daily Values are based on a 2,000 calorie diet.

THANKS FOR READING! NOW LET'S TRY SOME **SUSHI** AND **DUMP DINNERS**....

http://bit.ly/2443TFg

To grab this **box set** simply follow the link mentioned above, or tap the book cover.

This will take you to a page where you can simply enter your email address and a PDF version of the **box set** will be emailed to you.

I hope you are ready for some serious cooking!

http://bit.ly/2443TFg

You will also receive updates about all my new books when they are free.

Also don't forget to like and subscribe on the social networks. I love meeting my readers. Links to all my profiles are below so please click and connect :)

Facebook

Twitter

COME ON…
LET'S BE FRIENDS :)

I adore my readers and love connecting with them socially. Please follow the links below so we can connect on Facebook, Twitter, and Google+.

Facebook

Twitter

I also have a blog that I regularly update for my readers so check it out below.

My Blog

Can I Ask A Favour?

If you found this book interesting, or have otherwise found any benefit in it. Then may I ask that you post a review of it on Amazon? Nothing excites me more than new reviews, especially reviews which suggest new topics for writing. I do read all reviews and I always factor feedback into my newer works.

So if you are willing to take ten minutes to write what you sincerely thought about this book then please visit our Amazon page and post your opinions.

Again thank you!

INTERESTED IN OTHER EASY COOKBOOKS?

Everything is easy! Check out my Amazon Author page for more great cookbooks:

For a complete listing of all my books please see my author page.

Printed in Great Britain
by Amazon